WHAT I KNOW FOR CERTAIN

Marika Rea

Mrs. Appleberry Press

Copyright © 2025 Marika Rea

All rights reserved.

No part of this publication may be reproduced, stored in a retrieval system, or transmitted in any form or by any means- electronic, mechanical, photocopying, recording, or otherwise- without the prior written permission of the publisher, except in the case of brief quotations used in reviews or articles.

First edition, 2025

Illustrations by Author- assisted by AI.

For Fionn, even oceans apart,
you are never out of my heart,
and for Nan, whose love
carries across every wave.

Author Note

Sometimes, my own heart feels a little wobbly, and the world seems to turn too fast.

So, I wrote this book for you because I know that feeling too.

This story is a small, quiet space we share.

It's a secret reminder that even when everything else is moving, the feeling of a loving hand in yours is a perfect, certain thing. ♥

When you feel a little lost, just remember the dancing shadows. We made them together you and I. And they will always be there, a quiet, wonderful certainty to remind **you** that you're never, **ever** alone.

Love,

Your friend Marika x

N: Ships will always sail out of the harbour, and planes will take off to faraway lands but they go both ways. Life is one big adventure, and it's only natural to want to see what's out there.

N: Because people need their roots. A tree can grow tall only because its roots hold it steady.

N: Nan and Pop's house will always be a home away from home.

F: I loove it there!

N: That's because we belong to each other. Our hearts are tied together, and even the house seems to hug you when you visit.

N: Laughter will always rule the world and move mountains.

F: Move mountains?

N: Maybe not really - but it sure feels like it. If you can laugh at your troubles, you've got the power to light up the whole world.

N: She sounds wise. Imagine how lonely it would be if nobody understood you. We can step into another's shoes just by imagining— that's how you get human x-ray vision.

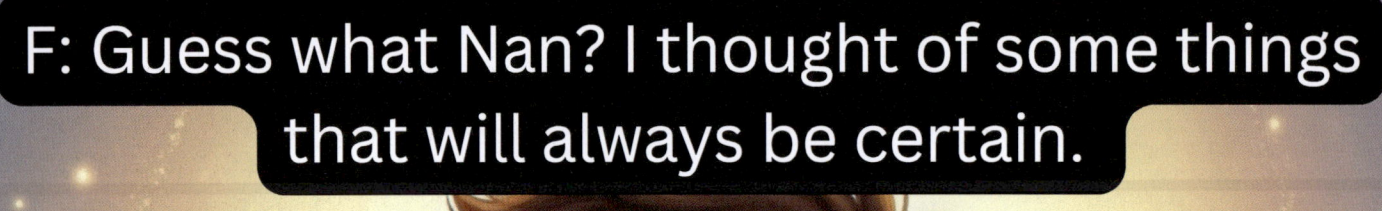
F: Guess what Nan? I thought of some things that will always be certain.

F: A day at the beach is always fun.

N: The biggest and most certain thing I know is....

Narrator: She reaches out and takes his hand, leading him to the wall just as the last light of day fades. A single streetlamp flickers on, casting their two small shadows onto the wall.

N: Come here Fionn. Look at this!

F: It's our shadows.

Narrator: She smiles, and a secret seems to pass between them.

She doesn't say a word. She just places his little hand in hers and looks at him. He looks up at their shadows, their two shapes joined perfectly as one.

Then, Nan does a little dance, and their shadow dances too. She makes her shadow a bird, then a tree, and then a cloud. He giggles and makes his shadow a dog, then a monster.

In the small dimly lit space between them, their shadows become a playground - a secret world that only they can see. And in that moment, in the quiet, certain joy of her hand in his and their dancing shadows on the wall, he knows...

What I Know for Certain Checklist
Write your own....

I know for certain that....

A sound that makes me happy is....

A feeling that makes me safe is....

A Note for the Grown-ups

From a heart that knows to another, this book was written for you as much as it was for your child.
When the world feels too big, too fast, or too full of noise, it can be hard to remember that some things are still certain.

The beautiful mess of anxiety can make a person feel untethered, as if nothing can be trusted to stay the same. This book is for the little ones who feel that way. The love between Fionn and his Nan is an anchor. It's a quiet, perfect truth that no amount of change can shake. My hope is that the story of their dancing shadows will give your child a new way to see the world, to find their own small, unshakeable truths that bring comfort and calm.

After you finish reading, I encourage you to close your eyes with your child and ask them 'What is something you know for certain?' It might be the feel of their favourite blanket, the taste of a cookie, or the sound of the rain. In those small, honest answers, you will both find the certainty you need.

Thanks for reading

If you enjoyed this book, please leave a review on Amazon and help other kids discover this story.

Other titles by Marika Rea:

Now on Amazon. Check out my website www.mrsappleberrypress.ie for more details.

Children's Books
Fiorella Can't Jump
The Boy Who Followed Me
Greedy Little Marnie
and Her Weird Smelly Bag
Taka the Wolf
The Girl Whose Hair
Wouldn't Grow

Printed in Dunstable, United Kingdom